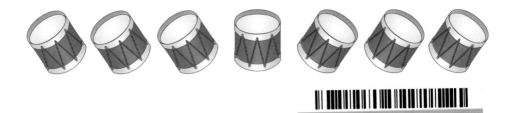

Distant Drums, Different Drummers

A Guide for Young People with ADHD

■ ■ ■ ◆ ■ ■ ■

Barbara D. Ingersoll, Ph.D.

Book Design by Anne Dougherty • Illustration by Karen Henrickson Sothoron

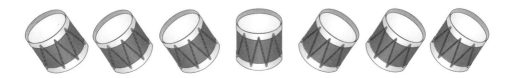

Published by Cape Publications, Incorporated

Reproduction or translation of any part of this work beyond that permitted by Section 107 or 108 of the 1976 United States Copyright Act without the permission of the copyright owner is unlawful. Requests for permission or further information should be addressed to: Cape Publications, Inc., 4838 Park Avenue, Bethesda, Maryland 20816.

Library of Congress Cataloging-in-Publication data

Ingersoll, Barbara D., 1945 –
    Distant Drums, Different Drummers: A Guide for Young People with ADHD / Barbara D. Ingersoll – 1st ed.

            p. cm.

    "An identification of the generic traits characterizing a positive explanation of the origins of attention deficit hyperactivity disorder (ADHD) for children and adolescents."

    1. Attention deficit hyperactivity disorder – popular works.
    2. hyperactive children.

I. title.

ISBN #0-9648548-0-5

10   9   8   7   6   5   4   3   2

AUTHOR'S NOTE

More than a decade ago, I had the privilege of working with Dr. Karen Levitis, a dedicated pediatrician with expertise in ADHD. Dr. Levitis saw children and adolescents with ADHD, not as troubled or difficult young people, but as modern-day descendants of bold and daring adventurers of long ago. Her perspective helped shape my own thinking – and sowed the seeds of this book. I am also grateful to my friend and colleague, Dr. Sam Goldstein, for his critical thinking and his astute comments.

Distant Drums, Different Drummers

Distant Drums, Different Drummers

■ ■ ■ ◆ ■ ■ ■

*Since you are reading this book, it's a safe bet
that you have been told that you have Attention Deficit
Hyperactivity Disorder — or ADHD,
as it's usually called for short.*

When you learned that you had ADHD, perhaps you thought you had some weird disease. Maybe you felt like you were the only one in the world with problems like yours. But if you have ADHD, you are certainly not alone. Scientists who study ADHD tell us that at least one out of every twenty people in the United States under the age of eighteen has ADHD. That means that:

> *if there are twenty-five students in your class at school, at least one of your classmates — or maybe two — also has ADHD;*
>
> *if there are two hundred kids at your summer camp, there are probably nine or ten others, besides yourself, who have ADHD;*
>
> *if you go to a rock concert attended by two thousand people, there will be at least one hundred people there with ADHD.*

You can see from this that ADHD isn't so rare. In fact, it's pretty common. But people aren't aware of this because ADHD isn't like measles or a broken arm: you can't tell whether someone has ADHD just by looking at him.

And they can't tell that you have ADHD just by looking at you.

What is ADHD?

■ ■ ■ ◆ ■ ■ ■

People with ADHD have problems when they have
to pay attention to something that isn't very exciting, like
math facts or spelling.

When people with ADHD have to pay attention to things they find dull, they often create their own excitement. They may daydream about action heroes and come up with new ideas for exciting plots, scary monsters, or powerful weapons. Sometimes, in fact, they become so interested in developing new adventures or sketching new weapons that an entire lesson goes by and they don't hear a word the teacher says.

People with ADHD also have problems with organization. They never have all the materials they need to complete a project for school or for Scouts or for anything else. In fact, it's about all they can do to find their shoes every morning before the bus comes. Then, when they get on the bus, they discover that they have forgotten their lunch money or their back-pack or their gym clothes. They almost always forget to have permission slips signed by their parents, so they miss out on a lot of field trips and other interesting activities at school.

Some people with ADHD also find it hard to sit still for very long. They like to go out to dinner, but they don't like waiting for the food to arrive. And they certainly don't like to wait for others to finish eating when they are ready to go. They don't like waiting in lines, either, even for a great new movie or an exciting ride at Disney World. And they

HATE doing things like going grocery shopping or keeping Mom company when she goes out to buy new sheets or towels or underwear. In fact, they even get bored when the purpose of the shopping trip is to buy new clothes for themselves.

Having lots of energy can be great because you can have fun long after everyone else has pooped out. But people who are very active sometimes bother others around them, even though they don't mean to. Teachers, for example, get angry when you get out of your seat or run in the halls. Parents get upset when you leave the dinner table ten times in one meal or bounce in place on the couch while watching television. "For heaven sakes, can't you settle down!" your father yells for the millionth time. Even though you didn't really mean to cause trouble, Dad is angry and you feel bad.

Finally, most people with ADHD are impulsive; that is, they tend to do things without thinking about the consequences. If someone dares them to jump off the roof of the garage or take the family car out for a joy ride, they don't stop to consider the danger involved until it's too late — and then it is, indeed, too late!

Impulsivity gets people with ADHD into trouble in other ways, too. Even when what they do is not dangerous, they may irritate others by calling out in class, grabbing things without thinking, and interrupting the conversations or games of others. They don't mean to be rude, but their impulsive actions can make them appear selfish and inconsiderate.

ADHD: Disorder or Difference?

■ ■ ■ ◆ ■ ■ ■

People who have ADHD have problems in many important situations. School, for example, is difficult for children and teenagers with ADHD because there isn't much action in the average classroom. Most of the day is spent sitting at a desk, copying information from the blackboard or listening to the teacher talk about things that don't seem to have much importance for daily life.

Homework is even worse. After an entire day in school, you're ready for some fun. You want to ride your skateboard or play on the computer. But you can't: you have three pages of math homework to do, twenty spelling words to learn, and a two-page paper to write for your World Studies report.

So, what happens? You decide to do something that you want to do before you tackle your homework. But your mother has other ideas. You're walking out the front door when she says, "You're not going anywhere until you've finished your homework. Let me see what you've done."

You try hard to fake it: "I don't have any homework," you say. Or, "I've already done it." But your mother doesn't give up. "Let me see it," she says, with **that look** on her face. There's no way out of it: she knows you have a report due tomorrow and she wants to see it — **NOW!** Of course, you can't produce the report, so your mother goes ballistic.

The result? You and your mother spend two hours screaming at each other and three more hours putting together the report that you have to hand in the next day. The report gets done, but no one is happy.

School-related situations are major hassles but they aren't the only problems you face. People with ADHD have problems in other situations, too, like household chores. Can you think of anything more boring than taking out the garbage or vacuuming the living room? Since boredom is so painful for people with ADHD, they often spend more time trying to avoid the chore than it would take to simply do it and get it over with.

But, just because you find it difficult to stick with boring tasks, is this a "deficit"? If you have more energy than other people, are you "hyperactive"? If you tend to act before you think things through, does this mean you have a "disorder"? Or do you just do things in a different way — your own way?

Individual Differences: Different Strokes for Different Folks

■ ■ ■ ◆ ■ ■ ■

If you think about it, you know that people are different from each other in their interests and abilities. Some people have beautiful voices; others sound like frogs when they try to sing. Some people can draw anything they see and make it look exactly like the real thing; others can't draw stick figures. Some people who can't sing or draw very well are a whiz with mechanical devices. Still others can't do any of these things well but they write beautiful poetry or they can sink a basketball from clear across the court.

Which of these skills is the most important? The answer depends on the situation. If you're in the middle of a hot game against another basketball team, the most important skill is the ability to shoot baskets. But, if your car breaks down on the freeway, you don't care whether the mechanic who arrives knows a basketball from a football: you just want him to fix your car. Your English teacher acts like the most important skill in the world is the ability to diagram a sentence. But how helpful would your English teacher be if you were stranded in the desert, dying from hunger and thirst? Could she use a verb to help you find water or provide you with food ?

Does *everyone* have a "deficit" or a "disorder"? Or are we all just different in our skills and abilities? If this is the case — and it certainly seems to be — maybe we should think about coining a new term. Perhaps instead of Attention Deficit Hyperactivity Disorder, we should call it **A**ttention **D**eployment/**H**igh energy **D**ifference to indicate that people with **ADHD** don't have a deficit or a disorder: they just have **high** levels of energy and they **deploy,** or distribute, their attention **differently.**

Why are People with ADHD Different?

■ ■ ■ ◆ ■ ■ ■

*Scientists tell us that different parts of the
brain have different jobs to do. Some areas interpret
information coming in from the eyes. Other areas
specialize in interpreting information that comes in through
the ears, like music or sudden noises. Still other areas have
the job of learning to use words so that we can
communicate with other people.*

The frontal area of the brain — the part that lies directly behind your forehead — deals with the ability to pay attention, to develop plans to meet new situations, and to stick with the plan until the job is done. This area of the brain also serves to "put the brakes" on impulsive behavior that could be dangerous or that might get you into trouble with other people.

In people with ADHD, this area of the brain doesn't work the way it does in other people. When people without ADHD concentrate on boring tasks, hundreds of thousands of brain cells in the frontal region send signals back and forth at incredibly high rates of speed. As a result of this high-powered effort, distracting signals are filtered out and all attention is focused on the task at hand.

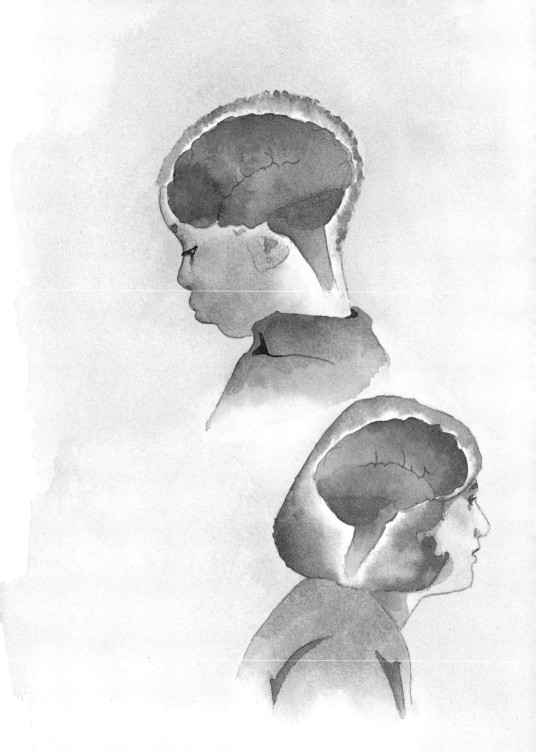

During concentration, the frontal part of the brain is less active in a person with ADHD (bottom) than in other people (top).

But, when people with ADHD try to concentrate on a boring task, this area of the brain does not respond with the high levels of activity needed to focus attention on the task at hand. In fact, when we look at pictures of the brain at work, it looks like someone forgot to "turn on" this part of the brain.

The frontal regions of the brain don't have much to do with intelligence so it is possible to be very intelligent yet still have a frontal system that isn't as efficient as it might be. Unfortunately, since so much of what we do today requires the ability to stick with boring tasks and to pay close attention to details, even very intelligent people with ADHD may have trouble producing work that satisfies their parents, teachers, and bosses.

What Causes the Difference?

■ ■ ■ ◆ ■ ■ ■

To answer this question, we have to go very far back in time.
We have to go back so far, in fact, that it stretches the
imagination just to think about it.

Our species, Homo sapiens, has been living on this planet for over one hundred thousand years. This is a long, long time, especially when you remember that it was only 500 years ago that Columbus discovered America. Even the great pyramids in Egypt are only 5,000 years old — not old at all when you think in terms of hundreds of thousands of years.

When we go back 100 thousand years in time, what do we see? Our early ancestors did not live in cities or towns. Instead, they were nomads, or wanderers, who lived in small groups of about 30 or 40 people. They hunted wild animals for meat and obtained the rest of their food by gathering fruits, beans, nuts, berries, and grains from plants that grew wild around them. As the seasons changed, these hunter-gatherers moved north in the summer and south in the winter to follow the food supply so they could feed themselves and their families.

How did these early people live? People who lived where caves were available used them for shelter. Others made tents of animal skins stretched over poles or huts covered with branches and the broad leaves of trees. In colder climates, early people made

earth-banked lodges within which several families lived together.

Although these early people often faced rugged conditions and hard times, they were surprisingly comfortable in their caves and skin dwellings. Since there were large herds of reindeer, aurochs, and bison — even huge woolly mammoths in some regions — skilled hunters could keep the tribe supplied with meat all year long.

Other parts of the animals were useful, too, from the fat that was burned in torches to the skins which were used to make soft beds and warm covers to ward off the cold. The hides of deer and wild cattle were used for clothing like shirts, leggings, and boots. In very cold weather, people wore outer garments made from the skins of heavily furred animals such as wolves and bears.

To turn the skins into garments, people needed tools, like scrapers to clean the hides of meat, fat, and membrane. They also needed sharp implements to cut the hides, pointed tools to punch holes in the leather, and strong bone needles to sew the pieces of hide together.

Tools were needed for other purposes, too. Hunters, for example, used arrows and spears with sharp points of flaked stone, antler, or bone. Special utensils were also needed to gather and prepare food: without pots in which to cook their food, for example, the diet of these early people would have been limited to hunks of meat charred over an open fire, along with some raw greens and vegetables.

Dividing the Work: Different Tasks for Different Talents

■ ■ ■ ◆ ■ ■ ■

Since so many tools and utensils were needed
for daily life, it meant that someone had to provide them.
Did each person in the little band make all of his own tools,
weapons, clothing, cooking utensils, and so on? Probably not.
Then, as in our own time, people differed in their interests and
abilities and it is likely that each did the work for which
he or she was best suited.

Some tended the campfire, stirred the cooking pots, and mashed the grains and roots for cereal. Perhaps while they tended the fire, they also wove the baskets used for collecting and carrying food. Others, meanwhile, worked on tanning the hides and cutting and sewing them into garments. Still others slowly and carefully chipped away at lumps of flint, shaping them into sharp knives, choppers, and pointed tools called augers which were used to bore holes into leather, wood, and bone.

And there were still others who, more restless and less inclined to linger by the fire, set off in search of adventure. On their journey, these bold adventurers might find herds of game animals, caches of wild honey, and rivers filled with fish. As they traveled, they also met and

did battle with enemies who threatened the safety of the little band gathered back at the camp.

You can see that these hunters had to have a great deal of energy to track animals over many miles. Then, having killed their prey, they needed strength and stamina to carry heavy loads of meat with them. This was not work for the weak or the lazy!

When these restless wanderers returned to camp with food, animal pelts, and other useful things, they were greeted with excitement by those who had stayed behind. That night, as everyone sat around the fire and feasted, the hunters and warriors told the stories of their adventures. The boldest and most successful of these adventurers were treated as heroes and from their ranks came the chiefs who led their people.

What made these adventurers different from those who stayed by the safety of the camp fire? Why were they more willing than others to take risks and face danger and hardships? Some scientists think that differences between the risk-takers and the stay-at-homes were due to differences in the frontal areas of their brains – the same areas that are involved in ADHD.

Could it be, then, that people with ADHD are the modern-day descendants of bold warriors and restless adventurers of old? Of course, we can't prove that this is true because we can't examine the brains of people who lived thousands of years ago. But scientists who study how man and other animals have changed and developed over long periods of time think that the idea is not at all far-fetched.

The Adventurer Through History

■ ■ ■ ◆ ■ ■ ■

As the years and the generations passed, there were great changes in the way people lived. About ten thousand years ago, people learned to tame and herd animals like sheep, cattle, and goats. They also learned to plant crops so they did not have to rely on luck to find ripe grains and fruits.

Since our ancestors no longer had to roam in search of food, they could settle in one place and build permanent dwellings which were larger and more comfortable than the skin huts in which they had lived as nomads. These early settlements grew into villages and towns and even great cities. Tools and weapons made of flint were replaced with sharp implements made of metal as people learned to mine, smelt, and work metal ores. Cloth garments replaced those sewn from animal skins. As life became easier for humans, the population swelled and people began to make war on their neighbors to gain control of fertile lands and rich grazing areas.

As these dramatic changes took place, what happened to adventurers such as hunters, scouts and warriors? Long having been providers and protectors of their people, they continued to be leaders in societies around the world for many thousands of years. At the head of their armies, warrior kings like Alexander the Great and Charlemagne conquered neighboring states and ruled vast empires. Closer to our own time, after General George Washington led

his troops to victory in the American Revolutionary War, he became he first president of our country.

Explorers, too, like Christopher Columbus, Amerigo Vespucci, Lewis and Clark, and Admiral Byrd surely came from a long line of adventurers: who else but their descendants would face the dangers of unknown lands and uncharted seas? Today, these adventurous men are remembered and honored by cities, rivers, states, and countries which bear their names.

The Adventurer Today

■ ■ ■ ◆ ■ ■ ■

*Times have changed for people who love action.
Now they live in a society that often seems to have no place for
them. Instead of roaming across the plains, modern trailblazers
and scouts may be trapped behind desks for long hours.
Instead of going forth to hunt game and slay enemies,
modern hunters and chieftains chase letters and
numbers around on little pieces of paper.*

Skills that were once crucial for survival often seem to have little value in today's world. Fast reflexes that served so well when quick action was needed on the battlefield now serve only to get modern warriors into trouble when they impulsively lash out with a fist in an argument or blurt out answers in class before the teacher calls on them. The energy that enabled hunters to track game tirelessly now makes it almost impossible for them to sit quietly during classes and meetings. The tendency to scan their surroundings instead of focusing on tiny details once kept scouts and explorers alert to danger; now, it results in what others call "off-task behavior" and "careless errors."

CHILDHOOD

Childhood today is difficult for adventurers because there are so many rules about what you can and can't do — little, irritating rules

like "Sit still at the dinner table" and "Don't leave your clothes on the floor." Rules in school can be even more frustrating: "Raise your hand before you speak," "Don't talk to your neighbor during class," and "Don't run in the halls."

In years past, active youngsters didn't have to worry about so many rules. Instead of being cooped up in schools and houses, they were free to roam all day, exploring the woods, the fields, and the streams around them. They didn't have to remain seated at the dinner table because people helped themselves to food when they were hungry — that is, if food was available. No one insisted that children sit quietly in the classroom because lessons weren't learned from books: instead, children learned life-skills like hunting, tracking, and fighting enemies by imitating adults.

Even chores weren't as boring years ago. If a child were sent to fetch water from the river, he might take a friend along or he might meet others at the river bank and stop to swim or play. Compare this with your chores today: how exciting is it to take out the trash? Unless you live in the Amazon jungle, your backyard is probably a boring place in which very little ever happens except when your dad goes out to mow the grass, and that certainly can't be called exciting.

ADOLESCENCE

In the past, when young people became teenagers they were welcomed into the world of adults with elaborate ceremonies and initiation rituals. Sometimes these rituals were painful and frightening, but they were never boring.

When a young person became an adult member of the group, it meant gaining adult privileges but it also meant taking on the responsibilities of an adult. Working with older members of the group,

teenagers honed the skills they had practiced as children. Work was often exhausting — even dangerous — but it was done in groups, so there were always friends around to share in the work and in the adventure.

In our modern society, classes, chores, and curfews mean that there is less time for fun and less time to spend with friends. Clocks and school bells tell us when to get up, when to eat, when to change classes — even when we can take a bathroom break. But clocks and bells keep their time, not your time: they don't care whether you're interested in what you're doing or so bored you could scream — when they signal "It's time to change to the next activity," you have to stop what you are doing and go on to the next thing.

In many ways, too, life is much less exciting today than it was for teenagers long ago. And, since people whose brains are action-oriented can't stand boredom, they find ways to create their own excitement. Unfortunately, the ways in which they create excitement sometimes get them into serious trouble with parents, teachers, neighbors — even the police and other authorities.

THE ADULT YEARS

When young adventurers become adults in our society, many find that life is easier than in their earlier years because they have greater freedom to do the things they enjoy. Those who are restless and hate to sit still take jobs which keep them on the go rather than stuck behind a desk — jobs like roving reporters or salespeople. Those who enjoy the thrills that come with taking risks pursue careers and hobbies that provide the excitement they love. Some, for example, become fire-fighters or police officers; others may work at desk jobs during the week and spend their weekends sky-diving or white-water rafting.

But even adults must do things they don't enjoy. Many otherwise successful adult adventurers have problems planning ahead, dealing with details, and meeting deadlines. This isn't surprising: years ago, time was measured by sunsets and seasons, so a few minutes or hours here or there didn't really matter much. Now, our lives are bound by schedules of hours and minutes counted out by a clock. This causes problems for modern adventurers because they often become so absorbed in their adventures that they lose track of time, so they miss important deadlines and appointments. Their bosses become impatient and angry when work isn't done on time. Friends get annoyed, too, when they are kept waiting at dinner parties or in front of movie theaters. The result is often lost jobs and lost friendships.

In addition to keeping track of time, modern adventurers also have trouble keeping track of their belongings. Things like socks, car keys, important papers, and eye glasses have an annoying habit of hiding in strange places where they cannot be found. This wasn't a problem in the past since hunters, warriors, and explorers had few possessions to worry about: they could carry what they needed on their backs or on the backs of pack animals.

Survival Skills

■ ■ ■ ◆ ■ ■ ■

*You can see that life today can be difficult for
modern-day adventurers. Mother Nature designed
them to master the dangers and demands of a world that was
very different from ours today. It is no wonder that
they find it hard to "fit in" now.*

Fortunately, if you have an "adventurer brain," there are many things that your parents and your teachers can do to help you succeed in today's world. Let's look at some of the things they can do — and some of the things that you can do to help yourself.

MEDICINE: FINE-TUNING THE BRAIN

People who love adventure, action and excitement have trouble when they must pay attention to work which they find boring. Certain kinds of medicines, like Ritalin and Dexedrine, can "turn on" the frontal parts of the brain so that it is easier to concentrate and finish tasks. These medicines help the brain's natural chemical messengers so that brain cells in frontal areas can communicate more efficiently with each other.

When these medicines are prescribed by your doctor, they are safe — quite unlike illegal drugs which are harmful and dangerous. But, even though medicine sounds promising, you might be reluctant to try it. Perhaps you're afraid that the medicine will take control

of you and change your personality so that you're not really yourself anymore. No one wants to feel controlled, like a robot, and that certainly isn't how these medications work. Instead, they help you control yourself so you can listen, pay attention, and think about what you need to do to solve problems in the classroom, in your home, and with your friends.

Maybe you worry that other kids will tease you if they find out that you take medicine. They might — it's true. But, think about the sort of people who would do that. Would you make fun of someone for wearing glasses or braces or for taking allergy medicine? If someone did that, would you want him for a friend? Or would you just think "What a jerk!" and avoid him?

Or maybe you just feel uneasy about using medicine to help you: you'd rather do everything on your own, even if it's a struggle. This independent attitude is great but sometimes it makes better sense to take advantage of things that are available if they can help you. Think about things like glasses for poor vision and nose-drops for a bad cold: you could live without them if you had to but isn't it nice to have them available if you need them?

SUPPORTIVE SURROUNDINGS: CREATING CONDITIONS FOR SUCCESS

We can't go back to the past and we can't bring back the kind of world in which hunters, explorers and other adventurers fared so well. But we can do many things to make our world a more user-friendly place for their modern-day descendants. Parents and teachers can help enormously by providing a setting in which you and other young people with ADHD are at your best, not your worst. They can, for example:

■ Help you organize yourself. Your room should have sturdy furniture and good storage areas so you can find things quickly when you need them. Lists can help you remember the things you need to do each night to get ready for school the next day. Since it's hard for you to remember to take home all of the books you need for your homework, your parents can make things easier by buying a second set of textbooks to keep at home.   They can also help by going through your backpack with you every day to be sure that you are organized and ready for the next day and for the day after that.

■ Recognize your wonderful energy and curiosity. Parents and teachers must also remember that it is hard for you to sit still. You need opportunities to move around during work-time and the chance to use up some of your extra energy in fun ways. Physical exercise helps, but it isn't always enough: riding your bike around the block twenty times isn't fun or exciting — it's just hard work.

Your parents should also remember that new places bring out the explorer in you, so you may dart away in malls and amusement parks when something catches your attention. In stores, you are so curious that you can't just look at things; you need to touch them, poke them, smell them, and play with them. Although you don't mean any harm, you sometimes break or damage things, so sales clerks act nervous and your parents get angry.

Parents of young hunters and warriors need to plan ahead to deal with problem situations. When they must go someplace that brings out the explorer or the daredevil in you, they should make arrangements to leave you with friends or with a sitter, if possible. You will be happier, and so will they. If you must go with them, the trip should be kept

short. Young adventurers also need to review the rules for behavior in the upcoming situation. If, for example, you're headed to the grocery store with your parents, the rules might include things like " Walk next to Mom — don't race up and down the aisles" and "Keep your hands in your pockets and don't touch things."

■ Help you stay on-task. Action-loving adventurers hate to even think about boring tasks. In fact, they dread them so much that they often dilly-dally, shilly-shally, and generally fool around instead of focusing on the tasks. The result? Work which should only take a few minutes takes an hour or two or three, with lots of screams from Mom along the way.

Since the sooner you're done, the sooner you can have fun, it makes sense to finish your work as quickly as possible. How can you speed yourself up and still do good work? Kitchen timers can help you keep your mind on your work so that you can work more efficiently. So can attention tapes* — audio cassette tapes that remind you to keep working instead of daydreaming or getting up to pet the cat or look out of the window.

■ Signal you when trouble looms. Sometimes you're just having fun poking your brother or bugging your mom and, before you know it — WHAM: you've gone too far and you're in trouble. Your parents and teachers could help by using signals to let you know when you're getting too close to the edge. For example, you and your teacher could agree that she will call your name and touch her ear to let you know that it's time to stop what you're doing, take a deep breath, and get your act together — fast. That way, you're not embarrassed by being criticized in front of the whole class.

*You can order such a tape, called the "Listen, Look, and Think Program," from the A.D.D. Warehouse (1-800-233-9273).

HELPING YOURSELF TO SUCCESS

Your parents and teachers can do a lot to help you, but they can only do part of the job. The rest you must do for yourself. Before you can **help** yourself, you have to **know** yourself. You can't work on your weak areas or take advantage of your strong points unless you know what they are.

To help you recognize your strong points and weak points, look at the Self-Rating Scale on the next two pages. Read each item on the list and decide whether you do very well in the situation (STRENGTH); whether it's an area in which you do okay (NO PROBLEM); or whether it is a problem area for you (NEEDS WORK). Rate yourself as honestly as you can. (You might want to ask your parents for their opinions, too). Remember that nobody in the world is good at everything. Trying to be great in everything you do would be a crazy, impossible goal. Instead, let's try to get a clear picture of what you're good at and where you need to work harder to improve things.

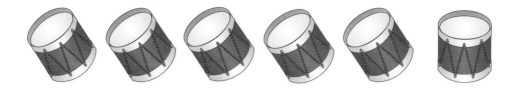

SELF-RATING SCALE

FAMILY

I get along with my Mom.
☐ STRENGTH   ☐ NO PROBLEM   ▣ NEEDS WORK

I get along with my Dad.
☐ STRENGTH   ☐ NO PROBLEM   ▣ NEEDS WORK

I get along with brothers, sisters.
☐ STRENGTH   ☐ NO PROBLEM   ▣ NEEDS WORK

FRIENDS

I get along with kids at school.
☐ STRENGTH   ☐ NO PROBLEM   ▣ NEEDS WORK

I get along with kids in my neighborhood.
☐ STRENGTH   ☐ NO PROBLEM   ▣ NEEDS WORK

I stay cool if I'm teased or if I lose a game.
☐ STRENGTH   ☐ NO PROBLEM   ▣ NEEDS WORK

I take turns and play fair.
☐ STRENGTH   ☐ NO PROBLEM   ▣ NEEDS WORK

S C H O O L / W O R K

I finish my class work on time.

☐ STRENGTH   ☐ NO PROBLEM   ☒ NEEDS WORK

I bring home books and assignments.

☐ STRENGTH   ☐ NO PROBLEM   ☒ NEEDS WORK

I get started on homework without a hassle.

☐ STRENGTH   ☐ NO PROBLEM   ☒ NEEDS WORK

I stick with my homework until it's done.

☐ STRENGTH   ☐ NO PROBLEM   ☒ NEEDS WORK

I turn in my completed homework.

☐ STRENGTH   ☐ NO PROBLEM   ☒ NEEDS WORK

C H O R E S & D U T I E S

I do my chores around the house.

☐ STRENGTH   ☐ NO PROBLEM   ☒ NEEDS WORK

I take care of my room and my belongings.

☐ STRENGTH   ☐ NO PROBLEM   ☒ NEEDS WORK

I get ready for bed, for school, and other activities on my own.

☐ STRENGTH   ☐ NO PROBLEM   ☒ NEEDS WORK

I keep myself (hair, body, teeth, clothes) clean.

☐ STRENGTH   ☐ NO PROBLEM   ☒ NEEDS WORK

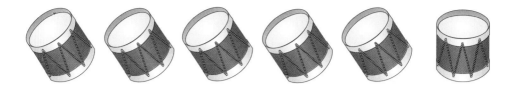

When you have identified your strong points and problem areas, you can think about how to use your strong points to good advantage and how to improve in the areas which cause problems for you. To get you started, here are some tips for dealing with the problems that modern-day adventurers encounter most often.

FAMILY: If you have problems getting along with your parents or your brothers and sisters, try holding regular family meetings to talk about the problems and to brainstorm ways to solve them. Set aside a special time for these meetings so they don't conflict with other activities. The rules are simple: each family member gets a chance to describe the problem as he or she sees it. One person acts as secretary and takes notes as the person talks. Everyone else simply listens — no interruptions! — and there is no debate or discussion until everyone has had a turn. Lectures aren't allowed, nor are put-downs, name-calling, swearing, or yelling.

When everyone has had a turn, it's time to start thinking about solutions. Come up with as many ideas as you can and write down all of them, even the ones that sound silly. Then decide on a solution everyone can live with. Since the best solutions usually involve a trade ("I'll do this for you if you'll do that for me"), be prepared to give something the other person wants in order to get something you want. For example, your parents could agree to let you have a friend sleep over on the weekend (something you want) if you keep your room clean all week (something they want).

Sometimes talking to a psychologist or another professional who specializes in working with families can help you find solutions to family problems. Some sessions with a family therapist can be

particularly helpful if you and your family just can't seem to agree on anything.

FRIENDS: Since everybody needs to have friends, life can be pretty miserable for young people who have trouble getting along with other kids. If you have problems making and keeping friends, you might join a social-skills group. In these programs, you can learn and practice all kinds of skills like how to join others who are playing a game, how to keep your cool if somebody teases you or says something nasty, and how to solve problems that come up while you're playing with your friends.

You might also think about ways to improve your skills in other areas, too, so that it will be easier for you to have fun with other kids. For example, if the kids in your neighborhood like to play a particular sport and you're not very good at the sport, you could take lessons or work with a coach to build your skills. Many summer day-camp programs offer training to improve skills in baseball, soccer, basketball, and other popular team sports.

SCHOOL WORK: If it's hard for you to finish your class work on time or stick with your homework for more than a few minutes, you might find a change in medicine helpful: ask your doctor for his opinion.

If you listed homework as a problem, it isn't surprising, since so many action-lovers have huge problems with homework. Maybe your problem is remembering to bring home all the books and other material you need each night: if that's the case, you should have a second set of books and you should keep a daily assignment notebook.

Another good strategy is to find a homework buddy who lives near you and is good about keeping track of assignments and doing

homework. Since adventurers often work better when they work with a partner, having a good homework buddy can be a life-saver.

It helps, too, to have a regular time and place for homework. Some people work best in quiet places, away from noise and distraction. Others seem to work better at the kitchen table, where a parent is on hand to answer questions or help solve a problem. Many adventurers think that music helps them concentrate while they work: if that works for you, that's fine — as long as it's music only and not a video or MTV.

SKILLS, HOBBIES, AND INTERESTS: Life should be more than just hard work, so you need to plan for fun in your life, too. In spite of their wonderful energy, too many young descendents of bold adventurers become "couch potatoes," glued to the television or video games as a substitute for real adventures.

Don't let this happen to you! Read the list on the next page and mark at least six things you think are (or would be) fun to do in your free time.

- ❏ Watching a video
- ❏ Roller blading
- ☒ Swimming
- ❏ Listening to music
- ☒ Overnight with a friend
- ❏ Building a model
- ❏ Going out to eat
- ❏ Taking a trip
- ☒ Playing a sport
- ☒ Playing an instrument
- ❏ Drawing, painting
- ❏ Acting in a play
- ❏ Horseback riding
- ☒ Playing computer games
- ☒ Other (fill in your own)

- ❏ Going to a movie
- ❏ Skateboarding
- ☒ Playing video games
- ❏ Going to a concert
- ❏ Playing a board game
- ❏ Going shopping
- ☒ Have friends over/visit friends
- ❏ Reading a book
- ❏ Doing karate
- ❏ Taking dance lessons
- ❏ Making things (crafts)
- ☒ Going to an amusement park
- ❏ Going to a museum
- ☒ Visiting relatives

Sitting down and Just thinking about Nothing inpartic ular

When you have a list of six activities, talk with your parents. Decide which activities you can explore, based on costs and time involved. Then figure out how you can get started. For example, your parents might be willing to pay for riding lessons if you agree to keep your room clean. Or maybe you could go to an amusement park or have a friend for an overnight if you complete all of your homework during the week. There are lots of possibilities for you to earn and enjoy fun activities: all it takes is a spirit of cooperation and a little imagination.

It takes imagination, too, to make sure that modern-day adventurers have what they need to do their best at home, in school, and everywhere else. If you and your parents and your teachers work together to help you succeed, who knows what wonderful things you might accomplish.

Your Hyperactive Child: A Parent's Guide to Coping with Attention Deficit Disorder

By Barbara D. Ingersoll

"In a style that is readable, entertaining, and informative, Barbara Ingersoll draws from her vast clinical experience with ADHD children and their families. She clearly, concisely, and factually delivers to the reader a work that, for years to come, will be a great aid to any one who comes in contact with children with this spectrum of disorders."
> Judith L. Rapoport, M.D.
> Alan J. Zametkin, M.D.
> National Institute of Mental Health

Attention Deficit Disorder and Learning Disabilities: Realities, Myths and Controversial Treatments

By Barbara D. Ingersoll and Sam Goldstein

"This book was exquisitely readable and contains information that is invaluable for parents and professionals alike...I commend you for having the courage and wisdom to stand and announce that "the emperor wears no clothes!"...Your text should sit on the bookshelf of every professional and child advocate in the country."
> Richard D. Lavoie
> Director, Riverview School

Lonely, Sad and Angry: A Parent's Guide to Depression in Children and Adolescents

By Barbara D. Ingersoll and Sam Goldstein

"I read Lonely, Sad and Angry from cover to cover — with increased admiration as I proceeded from one chapter to the next....It is well written, highly accessible and up-to-date. It covers everything currently known about depression in children and adolescents and seems to provide answers to every question that a parent might want to ask. The book should be of great value to every parent who has a depressed child."
> Editha D. Nottelmann, Ph.D.
> National Institute of Mental Health

Ordering Information: For your convenience, all of Dr. Ingersoll's books are available through Cape Publications.

Prices: The prices on the order form are subject to change without notice. Materials will be billed at the prices effective at the time of your order.

Purchase Orders: Net 30 Days. Balances over 30 days will accrue an automatic charge of 1.5% for each additional 30 day period or part thereof. Purchase orders can be accepted by FAX 301-229-3709 or by mail order.

Credit Card Purchases: Visa, MasterCard or American Express orders can be placed by FAX or by mail order.

Delivery Policy: UPS Ground is our preferred shipping method. UPS will not deliver to a post office box. Please include a UPS delivery address (street address) when ordering.

Shipping charges: For orders within the Continental U.S., see the shipping chart below. Canadian orders add an additional $7.00 to the shipping and handling charges listed below. International orders will be charged current shipping rates plus a handling charge. All payments must be in U.S. funds only.

PAYMENT INFORMATION

❏ Check or Money Order (Make checks payable to Cape Publications)

❏ Master Card ❏ Visa ❏ AmEx

Card # ▯▯▯▯▯▯▯▯▯▯▯▯▯▯▯▯▯

Expiration Date ▯▯ – ▯▯

Signature _____

SHIPPING AND HANDLING

Soft Cover
SINGLE ITEM $4.50
EACH ADDITIONAL $2.00

Hard Cover
SINGLE ITEM $5.50
EACH ADDITIONAL $3.00

NAME

STREET ADDRESS

CITY   STATE   ZIP

TELEPHONE

TITLE	QTY	PRICE EACH	TOTAL	SHIPPING	TOTAL PRICE
Your Hyperactive Child (Soft Cover)		$ 9.95			
Attention Deficit and Learning Disabilities (Soft Cover)		$12.95			
Lonely, Sad and Angry (Hard Cover)		$21.95			
Distant Drums, Different Drummers (Soft Cover)		$15.95			

MAIL TO : Cape Publications
4838 Park Avenue
Bethesda, MD 20816

FAX TO : 301-229-3709

Subtotal	
MD Residents add 5% Tax	
TOTAL	